Kittens

Alex Kuskowski

A Division of ABDO

ABDO
Publishing Company

Consulting Editor, Diane Craig, M.A./Reading Specialist

visit us at www.abdopublishing.com

Published by ABDO Publishing Company, a division of ABDO, P.O. Box 398166, Minneapolis, Minnesota 55439. Copyright © 2014 by Abdo Consulting Group, Inc. International copyrights reserved in all countries. No part of this book may be reproduced in any form without written permission from the publisher. SandCastle™ is a trademark and logo of ABDO Publishing Company.

Printed in the United States of America, North Mankato, Minnesota
062013
012014

 PRINTED ON RECYCLED PAPER

Editor: Liz Salzmann
Content Developer: Alex Kuskowski
Cover and Interior Design and Production: Mighty Media, Inc.
Photo Credits: Shutterstock, Thinkstock

Library of Congress Cataloging-in-Publication Data

Kuskowski, Alex.
  Kittens/ by Alex Kuskowski ; consulting editor, Diane Craig, M.A., reading specialist.
      pages cm. -- (Baby animals)
  Audience: Ages 4-9.
  ISBN 978-1-61783-838-5
1. Kittens--Juvenile literature. I. Title.
  SF445.7.K87 2014
  636.8'07--dc23
                    2012049663

SandCastle™ Level: Beginning

SandCastle™ books are created by a team of professional educators, reading specialists, and content developers around five essential components—phonemic awareness, phonics, vocabulary, text comprehension, and fluency—to assist young readers as they develop reading skills and strategies and increase their general knowledge. All books are written, reviewed, and leveled for guided reading, early reading intervention, and Accelerated Reader® programs for use in shared, guided, and independent reading and writing activities to support a balanced approach to literacy instruction. The SandCastle™ series has four levels that correspond to early literacy development. The levels are provided to help teachers and parents select appropriate books for young readers.

| Emerging Readers (no flags) | Beginning Readers (1 flag) | Transitional Readers (2 flags) | Fluent Readers (3 flags) |

Contents

Kittens

A baby cat is a kitten.

Kittens live in homes.

Kittens make great pets.

Kittens are born in a **litter**. They may not look alike. Their fur can have different colors and patterns.

Kittens start small. They grow fast. Kittens are cats after one year.

Kittens sleep a lot.

Maria's kitten takes a nap.

Carlos feeds his kitten
a snack. Kittens eat a lot
of small meals a day.

Sophie plays with her kitten Shadow. Shadow loves to **pounce**. Kittens practice hunting when they play.

Taylor pets her kitten Lucky. Lucky purrs when he is petted. Kittens purr when they are happy, hurt, nervous, or sick.

Robert's kitten licks her fur. Kittens use their tongues to clean their fur.

Kittens have **whiskers**. Kittens sense things with their whiskers.

Did You Know?

▶ A kitten's front paws have five toes. Its back paws have four toes.

▶ Kittens can see six times better than humans at night.

▶ Kittens have 32 **muscles** in each ear. They can move their ears in different directions.

▶ Each kitten has a different pattern on its nose. It's like human fingerprints.

Kitten Quiz

Read each sentence below. Then decide whether it is true or false.

1. Kittens are cats after one month.

2. Kittens eat a lot of small meals a day.

3. Shadow loves to **pounce**.

4. Kittens use their tongues to clean their fur.

5. Kittens cannot sense things with their **whiskers**.

Answers: 1. False   2. True   3. True   4. True   5. False

Glossary

litter – a group of baby animals, such as kittens, born at the same time.

muscle – the tissue connected to the bones that allows body parts to move.

pounce – to jump suddenly on something in order to catch it.

whisker – one of the long hairs around the mouth of an animal.